D1116961

*I Remember the Room Was Filled with Light*

THE WESLEYAN POETRY PROGRAM: VOLUME 66

# I Remember the Room Was Filled with Light

by

JUDITH HEMSCHEMEYER

*Wesleyan University Press*

MIDDLETOWN, CONNECTICUT

Acknowledgement is gratefully made to *The Beloit Poetry Journal, The Carleton Miscellany, The Hudson Review, The Kenyon Review, Southwest Review, Transatlantic Review,* and *The Western Humanities Review,* in the pages of which some of the poems in this book were first published.

Library of Congress Cataloging in Publication Data

Hemschemeyer, Judith.
    I remember the room was filled with light.

    (The Wesleyan poetry program, v. 66)
    Poems.
    I. Title.
PS3558.E479512          811'.5'4         72-11055
ISBN 0-8195-2066-7
ISBN 0-8195-1066-1 (pbk)

*Manufactured in the United States of America*
*First edition*

*This book is dedicated to the two people who encouraged me from the beginning, my husband Morton Rosenfeld and my friend Patricia Locke Towers.*

# Contents

*I Remember the Room Was Filled with Light*

# *Introit*

The old Eskimo method
Of naming a child was this:
Names were shouted in the room
Of the woman in her labor
And when the child heard his name called
He knew it and leaped from the womb.

So I hurl bits of past joy,
Past pain at my heart, to make
Meaning leap alive into
The light. Give up. How can I write
A song about the fear I feel
When I stare at my hands too long?

I flip through my loves like slides.
Absurd. How explain passion
That sprang from the *cruel* way
Her red pencil slashed through a word?
His clumsiness unbuttoning
My coat that long ago cold day?

Dreams? One of the Notre Dame
Gargoyles is slipping. Its thick
Stone thighs scramble, then slide down.
I walk in a brick-walled garden;
Huge warm bubbles form on the flowers,
Fusing, dividing endlessly.

Pollen spins in them like sperm.
I hug the earth, hoping each
Time for the perfect child: smooth,
Independent, wise, wild. But I
Might be that woman I met in Greece,
So crippled she couldn't give birth.

The child died and was cut and
Taken from her piece by piece.

# I Remember the Room Was Filled with Light

They were still young, younger than I am now.
I remember the room was filled with light
And moving air. I was watching him
Pick brass slivers from his hands as he did each night
After work. Bits of brass gleamed on his brow.
She was making supper. I stood on the rim
Of a wound just healing; so when he looked up
And asked me when we were going to eat
I ran to her, though she could hear. She smiled
And said 'Tell him . . . ' Then 'Tell her . . . ' On winged feet
I danced between them, forgiveness in my cup,
Wise messenger of the gods, their child.

## The Settlers

I was the father.
I crouched in deep grass
Behind the back kitchen
Turning the grindstone.
That was my job.

My sister was the mother,
Pounding grass for soup.
My cousins were the children.
They had to keep building,
Trampling the grass
To make more rounded green rooms.

No one could see me
But I worked until sundown
Because only the grass I had ground
Was real food, real medicine,
Real fuel to keep us warm.
In autumn we used maple leaves,
In winter, snow.

# Strawberries

The first time I went to the fields alone
I didn't see the strawberries until
I tripped and fell and lay completely still.
Then they came out. One by one at first,
Then clumped in constellations they emerged,
A galaxy of trembling, rooted starts.

But when I picked one and brought it back to earth,
My breathing on it moved it like a wind,
And it turned over in my giant hand
So sure of what it was that it could
Seem to be the accidental meeting
Of three glowing, polished drops of blood.

Berry, berries crushed against my tongue,
Broke the seal on a longing for sweetness
I didn't know was hidden in me.
I ate, reached out and ate. Chords of scent rose
From green, folded hay, my rolling body
And the red stains ripening on my clothes.

I whispered secrets to myself. I felt
The earth tip and the afternoon slide
Toward the edge as I stood up. So I ran
To the dark, inside place called home to bless
Beds and tables with my sweet, red hands.
But they told me I had ruined my dress.

# My Room

In nineteen hundred, when terminal
Cancer was thought to be contagious,
My great-grandmother brought one of her daughters
To a dark, Chicago rented room to 'rest.'
The last week the doctor made her put on
Rubber gloves. And the girl started to scream
When she saw them, felt them on her flesh.

I know. When I was seven I tried
To stop breathing, stop the stupid in-out,
In-out that made me feel like a fish.
My rage when I gasped for air was childish,
But so pure. Now, having taken shots,
Given life, gulped the bait of love, I must wait
In my body's darkened room for the gleam
Of a rubber glove.

# Rain

Rain in my town rained so hard,
It leaped into the sky again.
It made an ark of our back porch,
And we hung on the slats cackling
Like a pair of God's chosen ones,
My sister and I.

Lightning hit so near it rang the phone.
It whipped our mother back and forth.
She lit cigarettes, slammed sashes,
Ripped out cords and came, finally,
To cling to us in fear. For that alone
We loved the storm.

Then sun struck like a jungle knife.
The walk was strewn with stunned red worms
Packed dense with life as the placentas
We would one day glimpse. We jumped them
To wade in gutter streams as warm
As urine, swift as time.

# Encounter

One dead-hot day, when I was midwifing
Great ice clots from the fridge with numbing hands,
A boy-o crow, too big for the trees
And bold as a drummer, flew down to sing
To me, so close that I could see his fleas.

Head cocked, throat feathers puffed
Like a dirty ascot,
He swiftly manufactured
A manic monologue
Of low, sweet, rapid talk
To charm me out of crumbs.

Black crow, black Irish boozing man,
Just so, fifty years ago, you returned
To my grandmother. While you begged your skilled
Hands started on her buttons and she burned
Like a bride for the baby that killed her.

Old, *verboten* wino,
I saw you once in the park.
You shuffled with the pack
Of bums dwarfed by the elms.
You heard my cousin say
'That one's our grandpa.'

You stopped and peered with red eyes sad as Rembrandt's
At us, the priceless ones. You drank us in.
I had your dead wife's mouth; he, your long bones.
I wanted to wave, but my mother had to hide
The knives from you. My arm stiffened at my side.

# Daguerreotype

In those days there was no cure for anything,
Especially for love.
So she kept taking him back
Even though he treated her
Like a savage smashing a fine Swiss watch.

In those days people had gravestone names
Like Juba and Pergrapher.
Children died of measles,
So what chance had her twins
Against spinal meningitis?

In those days, watermelon pickles
Were called 'slippery Jims,'
And her name for snapdragons was 'breath of life'
Because their yellow muzzles gasped for air
When the napes of their necks were pinched.

In those days, when every pregnancy was like pushing
Off for Australia,
She had one too many glasses of sweet wine
At a picnic her last summer. 'Oh, my limbs,'
She laughed as she struggled to stand up, 'Oh, my limbs . . . '

# Snow

It wasn't the first snow that drove us mad,
But the first packing snow.

Not those delicately drifting showcase flakes —
Each a smugly exquisite arrangement
Of bits of ice surrounding bits of space—
But the first dense, all-day dumping
of tons of it, tuns of it
From a solid gray, wide-open sky.

By recess it was over our boots when
We spilled from the school. Paratroopers
Pushing off, we leaped, landed and floundered,
Tangled in shrouds of sheer delight.

Wild to make some kind of human mark
On that expanse of white, we fell on our backs,
Littering the schoolyard with snow-angel shadows
While the boys tracked out twenty-foot FUCKS.

But it packed; each scoop of snow could be compressed
Into a weapon, so we had to fight.

And we did. At first, playing war,
We filled the air with shouts of 'Japs!' and 'Stinky Krauts!'
Then, hit, hurt, suddenly enraged, we aged.
Grim, silent veterans, we had no thought
Except to maim them. And we did. The girls
Who couldn't aim crouched making ammunition,
Offering it to us as we rose, fired, ducked,
Rose, fired, ducked. We took ice balls in the face,

The chest. But we were ready when they rushed.
A bare fist . . . 'Look out!' Blood gushed from my nose,
But we drove them back. Numb, streaming with sweat,
We sprawled on our ramparts, triumphant louts.

From there we saw the stick-form teacher
Waving us in, but we didn't care —
It was our turn to storm. Each cradling a mound
Of ice balls we charged, leaped, tore their flag down.

We had won! Supporting our wounded
The way Marines in the newsreels would have done,
We slogged our way back to the school, an hour late,
Superbly exhausted, chilled to the bone.

We made our room a barrack, stamped our feet,
Shook ice clots from our hair, bared arms and legs
To boast our bruises. Radiators hissed
Our boots dry; toasting rubber filled the air.
And she couldn't do anything with us.
Our stiff paws couldn't write; books were absurd
To warriors clamoring to recite
Fresh deeds of glory. So she sulked at her desk
And we carried the afternoon away.
God, we felt sorry for grownups that day.

## My Grandmother Had Bones

My grandmother had bones as delicate
As ivory umbrella ribs. Orphaned
Early, she craved things no one could give her.
She boiled kettles dry and threw in her hand
If she was losing. No one outlived her,
But her health was never quite good. Her cat
Killed birds and made her cry. Still she kept him.
She loved green tea, postcards, things from far off.
'Where does the time go to?' she would sigh.
She went to bed, to mass, coughed her little cough.
She braided my hair like honey, but I
Had Mother do it over tight. Some whim
Made her dislike me, but I didn't care,
I thought. Why then, when she died, did I dream
She was a package of frozen meat?
Why was I chosen to throw her in the stream?
Why, when I had the bundle gathered neat
Did her raw wristbone scrape against my hair?

# *The Race*

Until sixth grade the Dutch girl could outrun
Us all, the boys as well. Then one day, amazed,
We watched her lose. After that things happened fast:
Their limbs grew sheaths of muscle, their crotches, guns;
From our ribs sprang soft white globes whose tips, grazed
By an arm, stiffened. Roughs of statues cast
From erectile tissue, they roamed the halls.
And when that bloody hurt hit us one by one,
With a shock no filmstrip could explain away,
Some girls swapped horrors in the shower stalls
— 'in labor, and the Japs tied up her legs!' Stunned
By the role my traitor body had to play,
I retreated to the Moscow of my mind.
From hidden towers I watch the dark Olympics
Of the bed, the bland face the O. B. puts on.
I know the myth is rigid, set. But I grind
My teeth for Atalanta, who could have kicked
Those golden balls and run, and run, and run.

# To My Sister as Lady Macbeth

It started in the mirror.
Your eyes cut such a cruel glance from it
That I forgot to cue you.

And where had your high-school hands
Learned to kill and curse with such clean gestures
That our house, till then tidy
And tightly wrapped around our mother's moods
As a purple cabbage round
Its core, was split wide open by your ranting.

Rebellion breathing on our thin old rugs,
Our kitchen chairs, changed them to
Richly patterned stage props urging slaughter.

She let you rave in your room.
Downstairs, I sliced stew meat with a knife
That knew it could sink into
The flesh of kings. We passed things politely
At supper. Our forks were slow
Even though poison was a different play.

That night they didn't know which way to look
When they overheard your wild
'Come . . . unsex me here' soliloquy.

In a week you were a polished killer,
Smoothly dooming high and low.
While I watched the pines and maples moving
In for the kill, you twisted
Your hands in dishwater to get them clean.
'Here's the smell of the blood still.'

24

You rode that blood right out the door, so proud
That even if you had known
What scenes were sprawled waiting in the wings,
Messy as the gore-smeared grooms,
You would have, being she, fine-honed your will
And plunged ahead to play them.

# The Goddess

My mother had a goddess for a friend.
Slim and brown, slightly hyperextended knees,
She could hold her liquor and won at cards.
Once she told how she was ironing
And her husband was touching the faucet
And they kissed. Wham! A shock pulsed through them
Just like in cartoons.

On picnics they made each other eat grass.
They had a little boy; they bought new cars.
They started running with a drinking crowd,
My mother said. When he told jokes that weren't
Allowed, I loved the way her head flew back
In smoky, throaty laughter. It was long,
Long after

That I found out he was a womanizer.
After he was red faced and hard fatted.
The boy grew up. She had the house redone.
Then one day she noticed that her arms were numb.
Soon they found her standing naked among
Her green-and-white-striped chairs, holding back screams
With both hands.

They let her come home for her son's wedding,
But she stood up and shouted down the priest
With babble about a dripping beast.
Now she won't talk to anyone, nor hold
Her grandson for fear that she'll drop him.
If they let her cook she gets cut and burned,
And she won't brush her teeth.

# Diary of a Decade

Ten years ago time tented me completely,
Each moment a gigantic, muscled canvas
Packed with the energy of conflicting options
Each screaming the uniqueness,
The brilliance of its own parabola.

I was a neo-Averroist.
Exulting in my discovery
That each strawberry is pressed to its own particular
Intensity of sweetness,
I crushed a cigarette against my wrist.

Now I have learned to let days flow like poured
Honey folding, slowly filling up a bowl.
Now I like children's hair warm from the sun, blue and green
    glass,
A light plane in one quarter of the sky,
The hum of its motor in another.

I'm safe home. I threw out that thin, sharp knife.
Yet I dreamed this farm: the barn fell away
To reveal a huge stone clock spinning in the dirt. I fled
Along lines of barbed wire, lines of Baudelaire,
Trying to read, trying not to get hurt.

# Triptych

Christ, now that I am the same age you were
When they pierced you and numbered all your bones,
Let me ask you: Have you heard the story
Of that eclectic French noblewoman
Marguerite de Navarre? So determined
Was she to ascertain where the soul goes
The moment the body dies that she stared
Unblinking at a dying servant's eyes.

Or how about the one the nun told us
(With a slow smile) to impress upon us
The importance of humility:
Two girls needing costumes for a masquerade
Wanted something super, something no one
Else would have, so they ordered fancy wigs
From Japan. They won first and second prize
And then contracted leprosy.

And remember what a fool I made of myself
During Lent when we were herded to church
To say the Stations of the Cross? Packed tight
We smelled of sausage, wet wool, galoshes.
The priest raced through the fourteen pastel plaster
Steps of your trip, the boys bucked like lambs,
And my will clenched to conceal from them my love
For you, but to let you, oh my Jesus, feel it.

## Some Days Are Born Clowns

Somnolent Sunday
With your bulging beach belly,
Toppling sand castles
With indolent wave fingers
As lazy as a roly-poly weekend uncle
Flicking his cigar,
Your lolling, popsicle grin
A meretricious, lap-hazard red:

Don't you mind
The dirty thousands of gulls
Parting your air in the middle?

And doesn't
Your sunning, butt-strewn rump ever itch?

And how come
You are always three o'clock in red suspenders,
Your flushed face already puffy
With the blue-hooed cloud cheeks
Of tomorrow's rain?

# Waiting on the Jews

There were none in our town;
They just didn't settle there.
The ragman came through and went away.

But June brought caravans of their cars
From Chicago. They drove hard to reach
The resort in one long, smooth ride.

There they opened up like calypsos,
Like orchids flown in from Hawaii
To shame our irises, our sleeping pines.

The men relaxed by playing cards for cash.
And the women, defying Isaiah,
Dressed to kill, then brought their scented bodies
Down to supper, using the rattan
Of the Victorian verandah
As a setting for their silks,
Festooning throats as white as columns
With ropes of fingered pearls.

Their names were fruit trees, mountains,
Roses, stars. The whole guileless garden
Of medieval Europe —
Green leaves, water, birds —
Was woven in that guest list
With gold and silver threads.

They gave me the Mendelssohns,
And every morning I heard music
When I walked toward their table with my tray.

('*Ach!* Felix is converting, have you heard?'
Clowned the professor, and the whole class roared.)

The Mendelssohns ate fast and laughed a lot
And the beauty of the breakfast
They ordered every day, the counterpoint
Of sour cream and prunes, made me imagine
Plump hands smoothing velvet at the opera,
Onstage a woman crumpling in a swoon.

Or did the swoon come as they drove away?
Just after he had tipped me and told me
Why she had to walk from chair to chair;
Because they stopped for gas one brilliant day
And she stepped from the car in all that light
And, dazzled, didn't see the cellar door
And so plunged headlong down a flight of stairs,
Completely destroying forever
The balance mechanism of her inner ear.

Or still later? When I saw
The synagogue depicted in stained glass
As a blindfold woman stumbling,
In her hand a broken staff.

Jews. All that light . . . They were the only ones
Who didn't see the diorama
Of their death in spun-sugar Easter eggs,
Who couldn't hear the starving string band
Sawing away in Hitler's mouth.
Jews. Light, more light! Dazzled by our guileless
Countryside they fell. And we watched them drop from sight.

*31*

# White Dwarfs

White dwarfs whirl alone. Wizened, burnt-out stars
Thousands of dark light-years away, apart,
Each turns on its axis only around
Its own collapsed, condensed heart.

Yet they are sending signals. I think of
Crashers at a wedding dance: drunk, despised,
Each in his corner clapping his steps, his spin
Of intricate patterns unseen by the bride.

White dwarfs lurch. At least the one I saw in France
Marching to church with her Communion class,
Stepping as if her cut-off veil
Could somehow float her dense, completed bones,

Already melting with the host on her tongue,
Translucent white dwarf of belief, her god
Who died young. What dance is this? What hard beat
Keeps all these white dwarfs spinning to its rod?

And gathers in their variations:
The faint, stubborn signals the dead stars toss,
The stuttering short circuit of the girl's
Creation, Christ's fading pulse on the cross. . . .

# Branca

Branca's eyes were as green as the Drac,
Her cheekbones high as unbombed bridges.

For most of the term she was a rumor,
The long-awaited Yugoslav whose room
Stood empty on Two. Empty, but passing it
I knew gray ash was falling endlessly
In there, softly filling up her mirror.

Then, toward spring, when the Isère bulged with run-off
And our dorm's giant beech tree,
Flaming with buds from trunk to twig ends,
Became a tender, splitting paradigm
Of all of France, she arrived exhausted.
Every year of her life had been breathed on,
Fingered, and finally stamped in some office,
And her low voice, still one country behind,
Scattered phrases of broken Italian
Like lost pieces of luggage down the hall.

She slept for two days and woke up starved
For faces, mountains, light, clouds, anything
Green, or French, bright brass knobs on old carved doors.
While I sipped her pale prune brandy,
She devoured the view from my window
And thanked me for the parachuted
U. S. processed cheese she ate in Forty-four.

Soon her room was filled with wreaths of twigs, friends,
And puppy pictures clipped from magazines.
We, with our muted prints, could smile,
But none of us could play the strict, no-handed
Hopscotch that she chalked in the passageway.

Her fiancé slept with his party card.
Only her grandmother still believed in God
And prayed in the house. But she was blind and scared
To eat the sticky prune tarts she adored
For fear of taking a wasp in her mouth.

And Branca? Somehow she had kicked her stone,
Leaped and landed in her own space.
Gracefully as a scalloped chain of wires,
She soared above her country's wild terrain.
Stubborn as a dialect or a river,
She found ways to surround and embrace it.
By June she was longing for strange-sounding
Sausages, for Belgrade's wide, cement heart,
For wheat, for solid fields of sunflowers
Turning as one, poppies orange as silk in heat.

The morning she left, already half ghost,
She came to memorize the mountains.

When the Nazis bombed Belgrade, she said,
She drew pictures of them with bullets for teeth.
And when they marched beneath her window
She flung it wide and screamed with all her hate
Some strange German words she had heard:
'Ich liebe dich! Ich liebe dich!' We laughed.

Then the train swallowed her up. I thought of
People with mist for hair, bodies of loam,
People passing by thousands through barbed wire
And emerging whole. I thought of Branca home.

# St-Just-de-Claix, 1957
To Claude

Smoothly, precisely as a swan's black beak
Meets and fits the snowy curve of its neck,
The small joys of life at St-Just-de-Claix
Suited me: tea at four o'clock each day,
You trying to talk me out of reading Molière,
At midnight mass the smell of incense and manure,
The sweet, ragged voices of the children's choir
Bullied by that ancient, crabby priest. . . .
Even the old woman found dead in her chair,
Her cats prowling round her, her face chalk white,
Seemed part of a plan to illustrate,
In rich detail, village life in France: a hearse
Of ebony and glass, black-plumed horses,
Lavender banners borne by acolytes.
Nights were so cold that one by one we undressed
Beside the tiny stove. To make us forget
The chill your mother told of her childhood
'Là-bas, en Algérie,' under the grapefruit trees.
And only the look in her eyes as she poured
Brandy for those two recruits who had come
To say good-bye, passed cigarettes to boys
Who would learn to hold them to flesh, revealed
That dazed France, like the dog I saw split open
In the road, was eating its own entrails.

# Dresden

The secret of porcelain trickled west
And revealed itself to a Dresden noble.
Priceless as the formula for Coke,
It was split in two. One workman knew the clay,
The 'bones' of it, and one the glaze, the 'flesh.'

Porcelain: Earth transformed to milk-white flame
Devouring jewels. Lustrous images of man
As shepherd, dwarf, nymph, bird-seller, clown, Jew,
Leaped from the minds of the *Modellmeister*
Into the soft hands of Europe's princes

And clung to the colored plates of our fourth-grade
Geography. So on the day they said
Dresden was bombed and the tide was turning,
I saw swans sliding off marble mantels,
Diving to death. Now I know the burning

Was visible for two hundred miles
And lasted six weeks. Water tanks and cellars
Were kilns where racks of quiet Germans baked.
Air was hot poison, but they sipped until
It was gone and death pinched their green nostrils shut.

I dreamed eyes bulged by tens of thousands, broke
And spilled down cheeks like botched blue underglaze.
The zoo flew open, too, and stranger beasts
Than ever twisted on tureens howled
At bay in the Altstadt's blazing cul-de-sacs.

For we were running the factory now,
And we were very strict. Bombs were our rods
And we were smashing all flawed figurines,
Stripping flesh from bone. Our mill ground finer
Than the gods'. Corpse crews waded in the blood.

# The Tailor's Ring

I have a friend whose father, a German
Tailor in the bowels of the Balkans,
Was tiny as the tailor in the legend,
The one who wore a sash embroidered
'Seven At One Blow.'

The uniform the Reich sent was a joke,
But he had his orders, so
He spent all night trying to make it fit.

Next day, trim, terrified, smaller than Hitler,
He tried to leave for Germany,
But partisans stitched bullets in his back
Before he reached the station.

And all he left her was a golden ring
Too small for any living finger.
Unbelievably small.

It ought to be gleaming
In the stinking, bone-rich soil of a mass grave
Near a castle, waiting
For the Nibelungs to dig it up again.

# Dürer Went to Sketch the Whale

Even though he could do marvellous rabbits
And had just won the patronage of Kaiser Karl,
Even though he had to travel by land
And by sea from Antwerp to Zealand,
Where it had been washed up dead on the shore,

Dürer went to sketch the whale. Because strange things,
*Seltsamen Dingen,* interested him,
*Er wollte also den Wal skizzieren.*

And even though he arrived too late,
The whale having been washed back out to sea,
Even though he landed in a storm,
Fell into the harbor and almost drowned,
Contracting a strange, nearly fatal fever
*'Eine wunderliche Krankheit . . .'*
From which he suffered the rest of his life,

He had gone to sketch the whale. He went home
To Nürnberg then, with his wife, her servant,
All their baggage, his beloved Bible,
His collection of *seltsamen Dingen*
(Bits of coral, buffalo horns and so on)

And that most wonderful of all strange things,
His own calm, steady vision of this life
And the life to come: strong as the thrum of blood
Through the huge heart of a whale, minutely detailed
As its network of arteries and veins,
Pure, copious as its oil, *geballt,* rich
And solidly animal as chunks of ambergris.

# Excursion

Patmos is whitewashed each summer by law.
It hurt our eyes as our caïque approached.
We climbed to the cool cave where Saint John saw
All those things:
The Horsemen, the plagues, the heavens peeled back
On the dazzling Lamb and dazed survivors
While a third of the earth lay scorched and black
And islands
Fled away. The guide monk showed us relics,
Which the pilgrims rushed to kiss: Saint John's splayed
Slippers (glassed), brown shiny bones, a stone pyx.
We stroked his
Pillow rock, walked the cliff where he stood face
To face with nightmares he called grace. Xristos!
Women were selling fish crocheted from lace.

# In the Mountains

The air was so thin
My mother's potatoes wouldn't boil,
And it only took two drinks
To make us high.

At night we slipped out
And climbed. Moonlight made us bone-white statues,
Our veins dark as pine boughs
Against the mountain's thigh.

Even our quarrel
On the path that coiled around barbaric
Hogbacks was ennobling —
Intense and cadenced

As an ancient play
In which a steaming, severed head is thrust
Suddenly 'aloft' and gazes
Blindly at the sky.

Then it rained and we lay
On Japanese pillows of raw two-by-fours
In the black shell of the block's
Last empty tract house,

Breathing new wood
And taking our slow way across those hushed
Minefields of ecstasy;
Faces, eyelids, skin.

Sleepy, our hands
Like stumbling brontosauri grazed continents
Of flesh, then overcome
By sweetness, sank to rest.

So we hardly noticed
When the room, the house rose from the grip
Of Colorado clay
And hurtled — freighted

Like a flimsy tomb
With all the artifacts we were to crave,
Rugs, silver, bottles of gin —
Brutally toward the day

Eyelids would be just
Dark hides stretched across the doorway
Of an abandoned cave,
Rubble heaped within.

We woke so cold
Our bones belonged to Eskimos, who carved
A dice game from my backbone,
A cup from your hip.

That way, don't you see?
There would always be fire, and faces
And warm hands to hold us both,
And you to hold me.

# 'If You Find Him Sad, Say I Am Dancing'

That whole summer — spent in a body
That was actually giving milk,

Whose hands learned to pull light levers smoothly
' . . . two, three' in the dark, illuminating
*Antony and Cleopatra* under stars
That tipped in view ' . . . two, three' on time each night,

Held rigid by the white lines on those charts —

Was a brash, wildly inaccurate map.

Dense with undecipherable detail,
Its boundaries trailing off North, South, East, West
To end in cloud kingdoms of puff-cheeked winds,

It had Colorado's foothills pyramiding
From Egypt's sludge, Elizabethan sloops
Dodging coiled serpents in the scaly seas.

You — acting in three plays at once — loved it.

But the language feast and postpartum
Chemistry were ganging up on me,
And I was becoming immortal.

Rehearsal by rehearsal I dissolved,
Groped for new bonds, then crystallized as part
Of every syllable he wrapped around
That doomed, giddy pair. One night it went so far
My breasts began to sting — Act Five, Scene Two —
When she pretends to give suck to the snake.

I slipped centuries. Rough hands passed me along.
Stripped, clothed in sweat, I danced for emperors,
Wrote Roman history with the slim hand
That dipped into the fig leaves for 'the worm.'

Ten speeches later I awoke to Enter
Dolabella: 'How goes it here?' 'All dead.'

I heard what he said. And ever since, though
The stars are still locked in those earphones
Attending the music of the spheres,
I have been drifting — oh, so gently — down.

## Old Photograph of Miners

They stand like a range of mountains
Bound together by some chance upheaval,
Dark, serious, one behind the other,
Bound to be worn down, cracked, smoothed, cracked again,
Sapped as they sap, undermined as they mine
By those few sweet decades — man's, miner's time.
Gone now the silver that froze in their veins
At the sight of a woman's taut throat,
Played out those gleaming nuggets of whisky rage,
The traces of shy tenderness behind
The solid shale of their pale, blackened faces.
Snow hides their cemeteries half the year
And heals the scars of tailings pulled from deep inside;
In Caribou one winter, all the children died.

# *That Day*

The day I found out you took all those pills —
Anything you could get your hands on —
I remembered my dream
Of the picturebook of animals.

A snake and a caged kitten shared one page,
The kitten on top, the snake below,
Waiting with its jaws hinged
Wide as the mouth of Hell in murals.

While I watched, the kitten started to squeeze
Its soft body through the bars and down,
Puncturing a corner
Of the snake's picture. The snake began

Its glide, lazy as lava. There was nothing
I could do. While you lay in leather bands
I stared at a stream
Until its banks moved and it stood still.

# Thin Musician

Ever since you junked your body
And disappeared inside your head,
I've been watching your eyes for some sign of you.
Don't forget the impetigo summer I spent
Keeping your hands busy — any kind of nutty game —
So you wouldn't scratch and make it spread.

And weeks before Christmas we'd play Santa,
You kids pretending to be asleep
While I sneaked in with toys in a pillowcase,
Clenching Dad's reeking pipe in my teeth.
You were never bad; you made your teddy bear
Say things to Mother you wouldn't dare.

What happened after I left home?
I know you started to send up flares;
Nobody is *that* accident-prone.
You tripped hugging bottles, set your arm on fire,
Loved music and smashed your fingering hand,
All warm-up acts for your grand finale:

A cycle crash half gravel, half barbed wire.
The scars from that — the doctors call them keloids —
Kept growing into more overt attempts:
Hepatitis from bad needles, cut wrists,
Then those methodical ODs; they say
You ate everything in the medicine chest.

Through it all, you never forgot my birthday,
One year it was an antique tobacco tin
Packed with raw nerves. Thin musician,
This year I'm greedy; I want you to live.
Stop pawning everything warm I give you.
Thin musician, let me ride on your strings.

# Spring, New England

The cardinal begins his song softly,
As if in a dream.
Something wakes him halfway through and he flutes it —
Loud, loud, steadily —
Then one diminuendo and he's done,
His territory, to the last half leaf,
Enthralled again, caught in his net of notes.

On the ground the girls are being readied,
Each tulip an Iphigenia,
A tender labia majora
About to break slowly into red-orange flame
So that the sails will fill, so that the ships . . .

Stirred by moving air,
New twigs cut the story in Greek letters —
Tridents, hooks and whips —
Against the sky: How a great shout went up
When the wind blew straight for Troy, how men fought
There until δεν ἔμεινε ρουθοῦνι
All perished, 'not a nostril remained to draw breath.'

From my doorway I can count seventeen
Shades of soft green. Fourth April of the war.
Mourning doves, warm wingèd grenades, shy past;
The cat wears a dead mole for a moustache;
Stooping, I gather branches for the pyre.

And down the road the old ones are washing
Their porch again,
Anointing its white posts just as her limbs
Were prepared for the fire,
Made fragrant with spices so that the sails,
Swollen by her screams . . . The cardinal
Begins again softly, as if in a dream.

## Eucharist

Skin is fine linen
Smoothed over marble
By the cool, worn hands of crones.

The raised design,
Crisp pubic lace,
So pleases the fingers of the priest

— He, who, with spare gestures
Calmly commands
The golden, sliding doors of the tabernacle —

That he angles the chalice;
The sun catches it
And the last he remembers he is sweating

Brilliant, concentric haloes,
The altar is arching to meet him,
The cupped blood stalls, turns to wine and aches

To dissolve the bone,
The slowly rotting relic
That such sweet sacraments are built upon.

## The Human Sail

Back in the days when the Navy was still
An orgy of textures — tar, canvas, rope
Brass, linen, wood, wool, crystal, pewter, rum —
A storm ripped every shred of sail from his ship,
The hundred-year-old sailor said,
As she rode at anchor in Samoa bay.
And she would have perished with all hands
But that the captain sent them up her rigging
And they hung on, spread-eagled in the wind
Until she came about. 'Eighty years since . . . '
But his palms still hold smooth ropes of proud flesh,
The scars he pulled from the teeth of the gale,
A human sailor, part of a human sail.

## The Chinese Woman Has Slipped into Madness

The Chinese woman has slipped into madness in spite of me,
In spite of the way my mind kept ducking behind hers,
Pushing back the boundaries of the permissible.

She would offer me coffee
But there are no clean spoons;
The children hide them.

Who told me she gave piano lessons?
That was before he ran away.

Now she writes. See, here is a pamphlet — *Sleep*.
And look at all the books she must read,
Piled eight, ten high on the piano.

Still, she should play something, just to show me.
Arching, bending, she lets the sonata take her,
Stumbles, insists . . . The kids turn up TV.

But the music was too much for her.
She stands trembling like one of those suspended kimono dolls
Boys put in their cars,

And phrases stream from her lips
Like bolts of silk thrown from a burning warehouse.

'I know six languages.
Six *European* languages.
How dare she show me the door?'

Her body makes dismissal motions.

'Sometimes I play all night. If only they . . .
I have certificates from Switzerland here in my drawer.
Drawers are for shameful things, *nicht wahr?*'

'In China no woman, no matter how poor,
Would touch the underdrawers of another.
Even the Empress has to wash her own.'

The children giggle. Why aren't they in school?
Why is every object in the overheated room
Suddenly slick with that brilliant poison,
That meaningless significance distilled by Dostoevsky?

Now she is ready to spill everything.
Her eyes fill and empty with flash after flash
Of brazen, unchecked, conscious agony.

Her hands try to thrust beginner's books into mine.

But I don't have to take them.
Were she an empress I wouldn't touch
What she is holding out. I flee

The blatting of the French ambulance siren
That ricochets off the walls and staggers after me —
A     *E*     A     *E*     A and flatting E.

## Something Is Wrong

Even though dinner is in the oven,
People we have known for years are coming,
The kids are at an integrated party
And we have just seen, at the museum,
An elaborate nailhead from a door
Of the Alhambra, smooth Zorach sculptures
And sketches of nudes with their legs flopped open,

Something is wrong.

Last week there was a fire in the A side
Of the building; but we live in B.
Down the hall, a child is being force-fed French.
I have a friend in California
Whose hold on sanity is the knowledge
That she is really a tan, fierce-maned horse.

# Heureux Qui, Comme Ulysse

*'A fait un beau voyage ...'*
But think, you sly one,
Of the clumsy, ruined monsters
In your wake.

You escape,
But they, poor props, poor paranoids,
Must crawl around their island
To repair

Those horrible defenses
That the gods can flick aside
For anyone wily
And fair.

When you came to our house
You steered first toward one of us,
Then toward the other,
And finally

Skimmed straight through
To more adventures.
And we crashed blindly back together
Like Symplygades.

By then it was long distance
And I felt my face pulled,
Against my will,
Into a mask of grief

As rigid as the molded plastic
In my hand.
'*Heureux qui, comme Ulysse* . . .'
But for us, a bad trip.

## *Walking Your Farm*

Walking your farm I came on troubled stones;
If I touched one, another would be jealous.
So I gave up and caressed them all.
Then some contour told my hands that inside
Each stone was a smoother, denser stone
That also longed to press against me.
Now you'll never get rid of me;
I'll be in your fields forever, waiting for them.

## At *Absolute Zero Even Alphabets Freeze*
## *and Fly Apart*
To Yevgeny Yevtushenko

Last week I dreamed my body inland,
Back to my small town. It was black night
But I was walking home from school.

Suddenly the sweet, curved lines of latitude
And longitude flowered in the sky
Like out-of-season fireworks,
And our whole Distant Early Warning zone
From Canada north to the Pole,
Flashed on this grid in neon-green outline,
Each obscure island x-rayed like a bone.

How safe I felt. For one thing, our DEW lines
Are tended by gentle, tireless Eskimos,
Men who could carve flesh and fur from stones
If there were money in it.
Second: I started growing,
And the bright defense web rayed from me somehow.
I was da Vinci's curly-haired, spread-eagled man
Radiating singing lines through space.

Then, just as I was getting the hang of it,
I sensed that three dark streaks, Russian missiles,
Had just slipped over the Pole and were inching
Across the glowing green of Baffinland.
Surely they'll be stopped now,
I remember thinking. Or now. Or now.
But slowly and steadily, maintaining
Their trajectories like three black drops of blood
Sprung from the hammered pressure
Of a crown of thorns, they keep dripping south,
Down Canada's vast and snowy brow.

Cut! I don't want to be here anymore.
My doomed retinas gag on the green map,
Then vomit it like so much neon bile,
And with dreamer's cunning I dissolve
Upward. A wind is cold between my legs.
A violet-blotched polar bear spins by,
Clawing at the complicated gas mask
Lashed to his streamlined, vicious face.

Then I am standing on worn, stone steps
Before a massive, carved, wooden door
Depicting simple miracles from some saint's life.
I want to study it but there's no time.
Newsreel Moscow is burning behind me,
For the first time in history without
The clanging of her bells to spread
Romantic panic to the suburbs.
This time intense heat has surprised them
In their towers, fused them tongue to barrel
And they flow, dumb and soft as Dali's watches.

I pound on the door and it opens,
Not to a church, but to Moscow Number Two,
The complete underground metropolis
You Russians have been building all these years.
Now, at last, I hear around me
The soft explosions of the Russian tongue.
Unseen, I watch the giant shelter function.
Everyone is slow, still kind, still calm.
Even children know the short war is on.

Only, near the door, one youth with classic
Slavic cheekbones is hysterical.
Laughing and crying, head thrown, back, he rides
In a pendulum sling that drags him
Back and forth through a trough of saltwater.
Then I see that his four charred stumps
Are still smoking, like ruined potatoes
Raked too late from the campfire coals,
And they are trying to cool him off.

I don't think it was you, Yevgeny.
Anyway, I woke up then, weak with joy
Because I tried to move my fingers
And it worked! because this winter at least,
Shirts will still be shirts; bandages, bandages.
And a night sky livid with light will be
Aurora borealis playing games,
Sketching leaps of dazzling simplicity
From horizon to horizon, and not yet
The other side of the world in flames.

# Gift

Let me wrap a poem around you —
Not now, when the curve of your life,
Like a mile-wide Pacific wave
Is rising, rushing you along,
Tons of sweet water supporting every limb —

But sometime, if ever you are thrown down
On some strange beach, or hurt, or so in love
With someone that you dare not make a start.
Then let me approach and offer you these words,
A poor shawl for your perfect throat.

# The Avocado Makes Its Move

My mistake to put it in a pot
With that exotic prayer plant.
I thought there would be *Lebensraum* for both.

Then I cut the avocado back,
Brutally, I thought, but it leaped upward.

Next they were neck in neck, the prayer plant
Accommodating its new green neighbor,

Tilting, angling its leaves by day — *So!*
To prove that there was plenty of sun,

Folding them each night, shutting the shop
As inconspicuously as possible.

How was I to know that all the while
Their roots were grappling like greased Turkish wrestlers

And that inch by cubic inch
The avocado was gaining adherents?

*Herr Wasser, Herr Nitrat,* all the strong ones
Come over to him, agreed to do their part.

And then, at precisely the right moment,
The avocado abolished elections

And made its move. No more of anything
For the supplicant, whose leaves each day asked less,

And yet each day lost thousands of stomata
To the advancing, crackling brown.

By then it was too late to repot;
It would have killed them both. In one more week

The avocado stood triumphant,
Two feet of green light and close-fitting leather,

Eager to please, straining like a dog
Trained in a language I only partly
Understand, ready for my next command.

# Skirmish

When you attacked with all the weapons I adore,
Wit, charming accent, classic fucked-up past,
Nonchalance bordering on cruelty,
I wanted to rush to all my borders
At once, throw in my best battalions
As the Yugoslavs did in World War Two,
Show you my dream book, my stare, *toute la boutique,*
Use others simply as steppingstones to you.
But I have done that before; each time I wake
To find the front moved on, my heart laid waste,
So I pulled back — the Russian technique —
Ringing my love's core with tough, tight circles
Of pretended calm. I won; I didn't fall.
Now you are gone and I am safe and cold and small.

# Dream Queen

Dark lady of the sonnets of my sleep,
Tough trail boss goading my nightmares, dream queen,

You've had me up on a murder rap
At least three times. Once I drew lightning
On an open pond and woke up dead.
Shrewd pimp, the same night I met that new couple
You put me between them in bed. *Touché.*

I can handle terror and straight gloves-off guilt.
It's when you hit below the belt. . . . Example:

My friend stands on a porch, that blue vein,
A soft, quick mouse, moving at her temple.
'If this vein runs through me, from head to toe,'
She says, 'I have to die.' 'And does it?' 'Yes.'
Or I am working hard, peeling potatoes
Close to Mother's throne. My lazy sisters,
Spitting toads, slink past crying out to the yard.

Free shrink, keeper of that dark, slimy zoo,
You sent swarms of thick green caterpillars
Over the sill and penned a huge, gold snake
For Daddy and me to kill with our brooms.

Aztec goddess, I've examined panther guts
To puzzle what hold you have on me.
Why don't I kick your snout when I awake
And send you reeling back? Instead I lie there,
Using all my tricks to reconstruct
Your latest cold-eyed rape of my self-esteem.

Dream queen, let's level. It's because I know
That only in your kingdom can I plant
A piece of smooth green marble and watch it grow.
Or walk down ancient Roman steps to bathe
In water that trails over me like hands.

And where else but in your house am I served clues?
Chunks of night knowledge torn from your dark soil:
'Time is a backward-flying vinegar owl.'

# I've Had So Many Chances

I've had so many chances
To make something of myself,

Fresh continents where I could have let my nails grow,
Stopped drinking once and for all, learned to dress. . . .

Instead I've bronzed my bad habits,
Solidified those splayed baby shoes

Precious only to me.
I love talismans, shards, debris.

For years I carried a cheap copper eagle
In the pocket of my corduroys

Just because I found it in the mud.
(Those black pants, beloved *tenue de pêche,*

A man once ripped them off me
And married me, but they're back, they're back.)

I have total recall. I remember
Each time I've been touched and why and by whom

Because it means too much.
I'd rather handle wood, sand smooth the surface

Of the design that throbs all through.
Sand with the grain; stay sane, stay sane. . . .

# This Love

This love is a bruise
Discovered in the shower.

The day I met you I knew
What I was going to do:

Wear green to dramatize my eyes,
Combine silence and wit

In measures calculated
To make you suffer a bit.

Maybe even become
Your 'secret sorrow.'

I thought I could handle it.
Ten thousand proverbs

Couldn't have kept me
From digging this pit and falling in.

Serves me right that you're leaving.
Now let the pain I planned begin.

# Craft

Everything is telling me to come to you:
Language-study posters from your land,
Your old car, driven now by someone new,
Runs over me each time I see it
In the      distance is kilometers *chez vous,*
Miles here, but twice our hearts were close enough to touch.

That's all I need. Working from shards
And comparisons I'll piece you whole.
You'll be my Apache basket, my Nimbres bowl.

# Like That Archeologist
For Donna

Like that archeologist
Who ruined his eyes
Deciphering inscriptions
In the desert sun,

I'm going to keep working
Until I break down
Your dead language.

Soon, centuries too late,
I'll find out
The enemy is advancing
And you are all alone.